Key stage 3

The Roman Empire

IAN COULSON

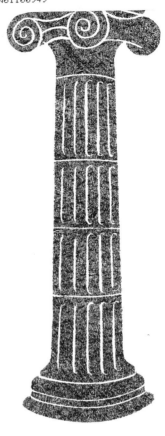

Oxford University Press 1992

Acknowledgements

The publishers would like to thank the following for permission to reproduce photographs:

Page 7 l English Heritage, r British Museum; p8tl British Museum, bl British Library, br Norwich Castle Museum/Alan Sorrell; p13 l&c Scala, tr Werner Forman Archive, cr British Museum; p16t University of Cambridge Committee for Aerial Photography, b Northamptonshire County Council; p17t St. Edmundsbury County Council; p18t Roman Research Trust, b Rheinisches Landesmuseum, Trier; p19t C M Dixon; p20 English Heritage; p21r Michael Holford; p22l Landesmuseum für Karnten; p23 C M Dixon; p25 c&tr Ancient Art & Architecture Collection; p26tl Michael Holford; p27 Canterbury Archaeological Trust; p29r Michael Holford; p30 Scala; p31 l Barts Medical Picture Library, r Hutchison; p32tl&c Mansell Collection, bl Scala; p33 Ancient Art & Architecture Collection; p34 cl, bl, c, br Scala, tl Werner Forman Archive; p35tl Deutschen Archeologischen Instituts, cl Werner Forman Archive, tr Mansell Collection, cr Sally & Richard Greenhill, br Museum of London; p36tl Scala, bl Colchester & Essex Museum; p37 Werner Forman Archive; p38 Michael Holford; p3t University of Cambridge Committee for Aerial Photography, b C M Dixon

Cover photograph: Scala

Illustrations: Peter Connolly: p40, p41t; Martin Cottam: p9, p10, p12, p14, p24, p29, p43; Bob Dewar: p6, p44/45, p47; Mike Williams: p3t&b, p26, p41r

Maps and diagrams: Technical Graphics

2 Contents

❀ Preface

This book is a study of life in the Roman Empire. It is designed to take pupils through the National Curriculum core unit by investigating a central question: *'what was it like living in the Roman Empire?'* This question and many of the pupil activities are open ended so that they can be answered at several levels by pupils of different abilities. In common with the other books in the series, pupils are encouraged to form an hypothesis at the beginning of their study and to work on the development and amendment of this hypothesis throughout their investigation of the various aspects of the Roman Empire.

The book is structured so that pupils start their study with an introduction to the growth and extent of the Empire. The central question is then posed and they are introduced to some fundamental aspects of Roman society and government. The chapters, beginning with *'Living in the Countryside'* can be studied in sequence or in whichever way the teacher thinks most appropriate. Throughout the book, pupils should develop their initial hypothesis and by the completion of the study unit they should have developed a more complete answer to the central question. The grids in the book are intended to assist pupils to record their findings and help them focus on the central question. Some time should be spent at the end of the unit looking at how and why their ideas might have changed and how this helps them to understand how history is studied.

The central question requires pupils to examine a wide range of sources and, therefore, several sections concentrate on Attainment Target Three, pupils' understanding of the use of historical sources. Other sections include activities on Attainment Targets One and Two. The headings in the chart at the back of the book provide a useful guide for teachers – linking the Attainment Targets and the Exercises.

Ian Coulson

The last Roman soldiers left Britain over 1500 years ago in about AD 415. For almost 400 years the Roman Empire and its leaders had influenced the lives of the people of Britain. This influence had lasted even longer in the rest of Europe and the lands around the Mediterranean. What was it like to live in the Roman Empire?

To find out we need to examine the sources that have survived from the period. They will help us find out about the people who lived during this time.

Opposite is a family grave from Roman Canterbury. This family was buried together. It seems that they all died at the same time from a plague. The mother and father have been laid with their young children resting against them. At their feet lies the skeleton of a dog, perhaps the family pet?

Unfortunately, no tombstone survives for this Canterbury family so we do not know their names. In some cases tombstones have survived. One tombstone was recently found in Greece. It was the tombstone of Tiberius Claudius Maximus, a cavalryman from the Seventh Legion. As a soldier he spent much of his life stationed in various parts of the Empire, until he finally retired after thirty years service. The tombstone tells us the story of his career in some detail.

A family grave from Roman Canterbury

EVIDENCE: ROMAN GRAVES

1 What can we find out about the family from the remains of its grave?
2 What other sources might we look at to tell us about what life was like for this family?
3 What clues are there on this tombstone that tell us about Tiberius and the Roman army?
4 What problems are there in using this tombstone to find out about Tiberius?

This book will investigate what life was like for people such as Tiberius and the family from Canterbury, living in the Roman Empire. Was life the same in Britain as it was elsewhere in the Empire? We will examine how the Empire affected people's lives and also see whether events so long ago still affect us today. First of all we need to discover what is meant by the word 'empire' and then find out some basic information about the size of the Roman Empire, when it began and when it ended.

The tombstone of Tiberius Claudius Maximus (see page 41)

What was the Roman Empire?

An 'empire' contains groups of people and areas of land that are controlled by a country or a single ruler. Empires are usually formed when one country invades and takes control of another by force. After a country becomes part of an empire there are often changes in trade, transport, the exchange of ideas and peoples' way of life. Things may get better or worse for the people who have been invaded.

Rome began as a village. We know from archaeological evidence that it existed in the Eighth Century BC, nearly 3,000 years ago. It grew in size to become a city. From about 500 BC Rome took over the neighbouring cities and small kingdoms, so it eventually controlled most of the country we now call Italy. One of the main reasons for its success was its efficient army. All Roman men who owned property had to be in the army for sixteen years. Every year they joined the army between Spring and Autumn. Imagine having to be a soldier in the army and give up the summer months every year for sixteen years! Why do you think the armies fought in the summer months and not in winter?

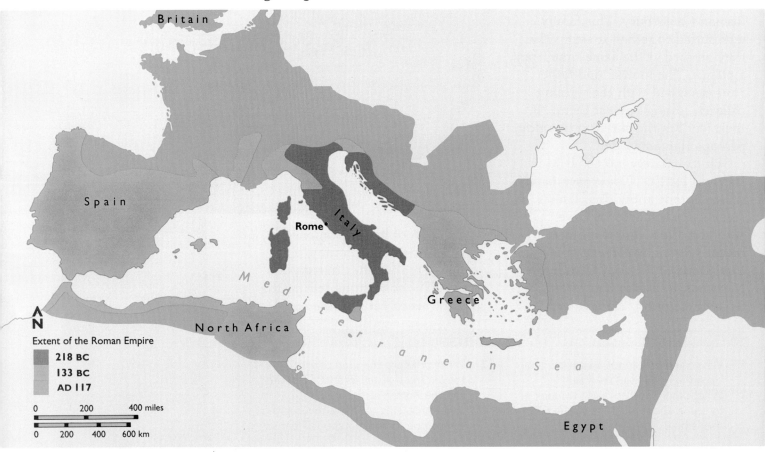

Extent of the Roman Empire

- 218 BC
- 133 BC
- AD 117

0   200   400 miles
0   200   400   600 km

The extent of the Roman Empire in 218 BC, 133 BC and AD 117

WHAT IS AN EMPIRE?

You may find a dictionary useful when answering some of these questions.

1   What is an empire? Write your own definition.
2   Make a list of the empires, emperors and empresses you have heard about.
3   Words often have more than one meaning. Are all empires controlled by emperors and empresses or can the word be used in other ways?
4   Explain the difference between an empire, a kingdom and a country.
5   What things do you think of when the word empire is mentioned? Make a list of the words that come to mind when you hear the words 'empire' or 'imperial' being used.

A Brief History of the Roman Empire

The Latins were the tribe that built Rome. In about 509 BC, the king was thrown out and a republic was formed. In the Republic the citizens, the free men who lived in and around Rome, voted for their own leaders rather than being ruled by a king. The word 'republic' means a type of government where the citizens choose their own leaders to govern the city or country.

After 509 BC Rome took over many of the surrounding cities and tribes. By 218 BC most of Italy had been conquered. This brought the city into contact with other Mediterranean countries such as North Africa, Spain and Greece, who were gradually defeated. As a port close to the centre of the Mediterranean, Rome's trade with many countries also grew.

In the middle of the First Century BC there was an important change in the way Rome organized her army. The army became professional. Its soldiers were no longer ordinary citizens fighting for Rome. Instead they were citizens who were paid for their services and who fought for the Imperators, the generals who paid their wages.

One of these Imperators, Augustus, became ruler of the republic in 27 BC. He used the title 'Emperor' and claimed that he was just the 'first citizen' of the Republic but in fact he made all the important government decisions. 27 BC was the end of the Republic and the beginning of the Empire. By AD 117 the Empire ruled by Trajan stretched from Scotland to Egypt. Tiberius, the soldier whose gravestone we saw on page 3, was in the army during this period.

The Empire did not expand a great deal after AD 117. Wars between rival emperors, economic problems and the halting of trade often stopped any further expansion. Peoples outside the Empire also wanted to move in and share in its wealth. Empires like Parthia and Persia threatened to attack Rome. In AD 285 one of the Emperors, Diocletian, divided the Empire into the Eastern Empire and the Western Empire to make it easier to rule such a large area. From about AD 370 the peoples on the edge of the Empire were being pushed into it by tribes known as the Huns. By AD 476 the Western Empire was ruled by Odoacer, the king of one of the invading tribes. Most people agreed that the Roman Empire in the West had come to an end. The Empire in the East survived until it was finally taken over by the Turks in AD 1453.

Date	The event	Explanation
509 BC	The first year of the Republic	A change in the way Rome was ruled

THE HISTORY OF ROME

1 What is meant by the phrase 'Roman Empire'?
2 a Draw a grid like the one above.
b Write down, in order, the dates you think are most important in the history of the Roman Republic and the Roman Empire.
c Next to each date explain why you think that date is important.

3 Draw a timeline and put on it the events that you included in your list. (This timeline will be useful throughout your study of the Roman Empire so keep it in a place where you can look at it again when we are asking the question 'what was it like to live in the Roman Empire?')

What was it like to live in the Roman Empire?

For nearly three hundred years Britain enjoyed in many respects the happiest and most comfortable times its inhabitants have known.

(Sir Winston Churchill, *History of the English Speaking Peoples*, 1953).

Many books and authors explain that the invasion of the Romans suddenly changed people's lives both in Britain and in other parts of the Empire. They also say that the Romans made life more comfortable for people living in their Empire.

How true is this? Did people really live comfortable lives in the Roman Empire? This is the question you are going to investigate, but how are you going to do it and where will you start?

Beginning an investigation

When historians begin an enquiry they often have a rough idea about the answer to their question. This may be because they already know a little bit about the people and the events they are studying. This rough answer is called an hypothesis.

You can form an hypothesis, to answer the question 'what was it like to live in the Roman Empire?', by using the sources on pages 7–8. But remember, your answer will only be the first rough answer, or hypothesis. As you work through the book you will use more sources. The evidence from those sources will probably help you change and improve your first hypothesis. This is not cheating! Historians do this all the time. It is simply the best way of getting close to the truth. You can see how this works in the cartoon below.

Putting together an hypothesis.

WHAT WAS IT LIKE LIVING IN THE ROMAN EMPIRE?

1 The sources from Britain on pages 7–8 give you enough information to form your first hypothesis. However, there are a lot of sources so it might help to record the information using a grid like the one opposite. Give a mark out of 5 in each box, using the scale below.
   5 = life was very comfortable
   4 = life was fairly comfortable
   3 = life was OK
   2 = life was fairly uncomfortable
   1 = life was very uncomfortable

2 Add up the totals. Which period was the most comfortable in which to live? (The most comfortable period will have the highest total.)

3 Write in your own words what you think it was like to live in the Roman Empire. Mention whether you think it was better or worse than living in Celtic or Saxon Britain.

	Celtic	Roman	Saxon
Housing			
Living in the houses			
Objects			
Written sources			

Celtic Britain   Roman Britain   Saxon Britain

BC AD   500

AD43   AD415

The British before, during and after the Roman occupation

The Celts of Iron Age Britain

Source C
The British are savages towards foreigners.

(Horace, *Odes*, written in the First Century BC)

Source D
By far the most civilized of the Britons are those who live in Kent, their way of life is very much like that of the Gauls (French). Most of the tribes living inland do not grow grain; they live on milk and meat and wear skins. All the Britons dye their bodies with woad, which produces a blue colour and gives them a wild appearance in battle. They wear their hair long; every other part of their body, except the upper lip they shave.

(Julius Caesar describing the Britons in 55 BC)

Source A
The Desborough mirror, made of polished bronze, late First Century BC.

Source B
A modern reconstruction of the inside of **Maiden Castle**, an Iron Age hill fort in Dorset.

Source E

A Roman vase from the Water Newton hoard, Fourth Century AD.

Source F
A reconstruction of **Lullingstone Roman villa**

Roman Britain

Source G

The people were unable to read or write, they often fought each other. So that they should become peaceful and quiet, Agricola, the Roman governor, helped them to build temples, market places and houses, praising those who wanted to do things and helping those who were half-hearted. They even copied the way that the Romans dressed, togas were often seen. Gradually the people got used to the luxuries – collonades, baths and parties.

(Tacitus writing about Agricola and the Britons in the First Century AD)

Saxon Britain

Source H

The houses were long rectangular timber buildings, often with living quarters for humans at one end and stalls for cattle at the other. There was a fireplace for cooking at the living end and wooden partitions dividing up the cattle stalls at the other end, with perhaps a third section in some houses which was used as a barn or a workshop.

(Christine Hills, archaeologist, 1986)

Source I
A page from a Saxon Bible.

Source J
A reconstruction of a Saxon house at Thetford, Norfolk

In the last chapter you began your investigation by writing the first draft of your answer to the question: What was it like living in the Roman Empire? Now you need to continue your investigation in detail by asking more questions about the people who lived in the Roman Empire. The key question in this chapter is:

∽ *Were people able to make their own choices about how they lived and how they were governed?*

Groups in school

HEAD TEACHER

TEACHERS

CARETAKER

OFFICE STAFF

PUPILS

People in groups

Your task is to find out what choices people had when it came to running their own lives. To do this you need to know how people organize themselves in groups. Wherever you find large numbers of people together they organize themselves. Think about your school for a moment. The pattern of organization will include a headteacher, the teachers, office staff, the caretaker and the pupils.

Any description of what it is like being a member of the school depends on which group you belong to. In the school organization each group is allowed to do different things and go to different places. For example, headteachers usually have their own offices whilst pupils have to share a classroom or tutor base.

People in the Roman Empire also belonged to definite groups. There were Roman citizens, freedmen and slaves. Within each of these groups there were men and women of different importance who might come from very different places and backgrounds in the Empire.

IMPROVING THE HYPOTHESIS

Think back to the questions on page 6. You had to choose the period that you thought was most comfortable to live in.

1 Did you mention that it might depend on whether you were a slave or not?

2 Why is it important to explain who you are investigating when you are describing life in the Roman Empire?

⬒ Who were the Roman citizens?

EMPEROR

The most important group of people who lived in the Empire were the Roman citizens. In the early days of the Republic most of the population of Rome lived on farms and not in the city. They were protected from attack by the army which they were expected to join and give their support to.

Being a citizen involved rights and responsibilities, some 'give and take' between the citizen and the government. By joining the army the citizen helped to protect his own land as well as defending Rome. In return for helping to defend the city he could claim certain rights such as being able to go to court in Rome if he were arrested. This would give him the chance of a fair trial. By paying taxes the citizen would support a government that in return would build public baths, provide the cities with clean water supplies and handouts of corn to the poor.

UPPER CLASS

EQUESTRIAN CLASS

ORDINARY CITIZENS

SLAVES & FREEDMEN

The number of people who could become citizens changed over time. About 100 BC people from the neighbouring states in Italy were allowed to become citizens. Soon afterwards the General Marius used the offer of citizenship as a bribe to stop states attacking Rome. There was another change during the Empire. As the Empire expanded more people were becoming Roman citizens. Britons, Germans and Africans began to speak Latin, the Roman language, as well as live and dress like the Romans. Soon it was difficult to tell exactly who came from Rome and who had been born in other countries. During the reign of Caracalla (AD 211–17), citizenship was granted to all free men in the Empire. This gave all free men the same rights but it also meant they all had to pay taxes. Citizenship was again a matter of 'give and take'. In this case Caracalla was desperate to take their money!

CITIZENS IN ROME AND TODAY

1 Who were the Roman citizens?
2 What were the advantages and disadvantages of being a Roman citizen?
3 What do we mean by the phrase 'citizenship' when we use it today?
4 Who are the citizens in this country today?

⊞ Who really ruled Rome?

In the Seventh Century BC Rome was a kingdom and the people of Rome were unable to choose their own ruler. Their leader was a king from another part of Italy.

When Rome became a republic its citizens chose leaders by voting for senators rather like we vote for Members of Parliament. The senators met in a great meeting room called the Senate. Here the important government decisions were made and the Senators argued about the best way to govern Rome. However, despite having elections Rome was not a democracy as we understand it. A modern democracy is where the government is elected by almost all the people above a certain age, who are free to vote for whichever group they want as the next government. To vote in any Roman elections you had to be a citizen. Many of those who lived in Rome, such as women, freedmen or slaves could not vote, so Republican Rome cannot claim to have been democratic.

There were several classes of citizen. The most influential and powerful were the group of very wealthy families known as the patricians. It was this group that supplied nearly all of the senators who ruled the city. These wealthy men from the patrician families had the time to work as members of the government and could afford to spend a great deal of money on their elections.

Elections should always be free from bribery (where people are paid to vote for one side or another) and from intimidation (where people are threatened with violence if they refuse to vote for one side). Unfortunately, during the Republic, 509 BC to AD 27, this was not always the case. When

each year, two senators were elected to rule the Republic, they usually came from the patrician families and often used bribery and intimidation to make sure that they won the election.

As a result of this corruption the citizens sometimes revolted against these senators from the wealthy patrician families.

In 40 BC the people of Rome 'banded together, shouting, and threw stones at anyone who would not join them, and threatened to burn down their houses. A senator tried to explain the problem but as soon as he came in front of the crowd they threw stones at him'
(Appian, *The Civil Wars*, written in the Second Century)

During the 100 years before the birth of Christ there was a great deal of political unrest in Rome. Then there was a major change. One man took control of the government. His name was Augustus.

Glossary

Corruption   dishonesty, cheating.
Democracy   where the government is elected by the people.
       where the people vote to select the government.
Government   the group of people who rule a country.
Kingdom   a country ruled by a king or queen.
Parliament   a place where those elected by the people meet to discuss how the country should be ruled.
Patrician Family   one of the old, wealthy, ruling familes of Rome.
Republic   a country where those who are elected control the government.
Senator   a person elected to sit in the Senate and govern Rome.

Roman Society
(Look at the figures on page 10.)

The Emperor was rich and powerful. He controlled huge areas of land, a professional army and raised taxes.

The upper class citizens were very wealthy. They were the senators of Rome and the governors of the provinces.

The equestrian class were wealthy and provided men for the government and the army.

The ordinary citizens of Rome could join the army or were farmers and tradesmen.

Women from poor backgrounds worked and looked after the family. Wealthy women were often well educated and had more independence.

Freedmen were labourers who worked in the towns or countryside.

Slaves could become very wealthy. Some were well educated whilst others lived in poverty and were badly treated.

⚏ The power of the Emperor

Augustus was supported by the army. It was the army that gave him the power to take over the government of the Empire and stay in power. Once he had seized power Augustus claimed to be going back to the 'old days' by ruling through the Senate who were elected by the citizens. In fact he ruled as a dictator and was known as the Emperor, a name that came from his role as leader of the army. Augustus gradually took away from the Senate many of its powers to make new laws and its ability to spend public money. More and more, it was the Emperor who made the important decisions in government. This meant that the Emperor was blamed for any problems as well as any successes. When the army was dissatisfied the Emperor might be murdered and replaced by a new leader.

Governing the Provinces

Ruling such a large area as the Roman Empire was difficult. Remember, there was no printing or any telephones so it was a problem keeping in touch with people who lived hundreds of miles away. The Emperors had to rely on the road system and transport by sea if they wanted to send instructions. Each part of the Empire, or province, had its own provincial governor, who was a senator and from Rome. Their main jobs were to settle disputes in their provinces, to collect taxes and to control the army. Assisting the provincial governors were citizens of the equestrian class who had jobs as senior government officials. The ordinary government jobs were done by freedmen or slaves. The Emperor appointed all the provincial governors and therefore was able to control exactly who was given the most important jobs. The diagram above shows the powers and the responsibilities of the Emperor.

THE PROVINCES OF THE EMPIRE

1 What was a province?
2 Name three provinces in the Empire. Look back at the map on page 4.
3 Write a paragraph about how the Emperors ruled the provinces
4 Which class did the provincial governors come from and what were their main jobs?
5 What do you think would happen if the Emperor was unable to control the army or his provincial governors?

The Emperor Augustus

Augustus was Emperor almost 2000 years ago. To find out what he was really like is difficult because much of the information about him has been lost or destroyed. However, some sources have survived. Look carefully at those shown below:

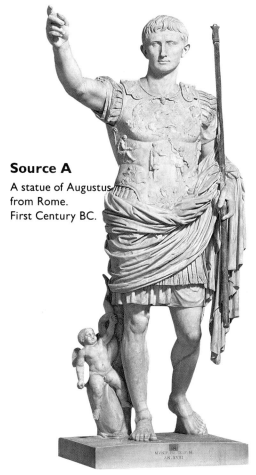

Source A

A statue of Augustus from Rome.
First Century BC.

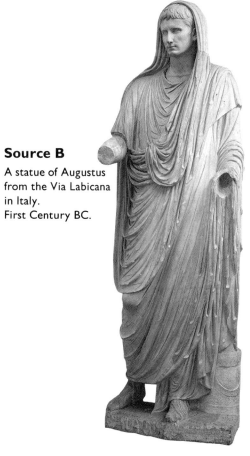

Source B

A statue of Augustus from the Via Labicana in Italy.
First Century BC.

Source C

A bronze head of Augustus from Sudan. First Century BC.

Source D

Augustus from a contemporary cameo.

Source E

After the second and final battle Augustus showed no mercy to his enemies, but sent Brutus's head to Rome.

(Suetonius, *The Life of Augustus*, c. AD 120)

Source F

The Romans have never enjoyed such peace and prosperity as that provided by Augustus.

(Stabo, written shortly after Augustus' death in AD 14)

Source G

He was a civil and pleasant man, he loved gambling and overslept excessively.

(Aurelius Victor. Written in the Fourth Century)

Source H

Augustus tried to explain the problem to the crowd but as soon as he came in front of them they threw stones at him.

(Appian, *The Civil Wars*. Written in the Second Century)

EVIDENCE: INDIVIDUALS IN THE ROMAN EMPIRE

1 Look at sources A–D.
  a How do they agree about Augustus' appearance?
  b How do they disagree about Augustus' appearance?
2 Sources A–D tell us about Augustus. Do they tell us anything about life in the Roman Empire?
3 What good things do sources E–H say about Augustus?

4 What bad things do they say about Augustus?
5 Which source or sources do you think are most useful for an investigation of:
  a Augustus' appearance?
  b Augustus' personality?
6 Write your own description of him.
7 What sources would you use to find out about an ordinary person who lived in the Empire?

⬚ Differences between Roman society and Celtic society

Celtic Society

The Celtic chief or king usually controlled a small area or region. They did not have professional armies.

Women in Celtic society were often leaders. For example Cartimandua of the Brigantes and Boudicca of the the Iceni in Britain in the First Century AD.

The Druids were concerned with religion, education and the settling of disputes.

Most of the population were peasants, slaves, freemen, farmers or craftsmen.

The warriors were trained fighters, usually landowners wealthy enough to own weapons, horses and chariots.

Source I

Little by little Britain became like the other provinces. A colony of retired soldiers was set-up at Colchester. Certain areas were given to the British King Cogidumnus to rule. This was something the Romans often did so it was easier to turn the land into a Roman province.

(The Roman historian Tacitus writing in about AD 97)

The Romans took over from the Celts in Northern Italy, parts of Germany, France and Britain. The Celts did not disappear but they became part of a new, mixed, society. Very few Romans from Italy came to settle in Britain. Most of the new settlers were traders, civil servants and soldiers who came from all over the Empire.

The new towns were run by elected town councils and they seem to have been able to make their own decisions and hold their own courts just as long as they collected the taxes for the governor. Most of the population of these towns was British and was divided into the same classes as the Romans: citizens, freemen and slaves.

ROMAN AND CELTIC SOCIETY

Look carefully at the information on this page and the Roman Society diagram on page 10.

1. In what way were the groups in Celtic society similar to those in Roman society?
2. Why were the Roman emperors so much more powerful than the Celtic kings?
3. Why did the Romans keep some of the Celtic kings in power?
4. Why do you think that the Romans did not let the warriors and the druids exist as part of the new Roman province?
5. Which of the Celtic groups do you think was least affected by the conquering Romans: the chiefs, the warriors and druids or the peasantry?
6. Do you think that Roman and Celtic society mixed easily? Explain your answer.
7. In which society do you think it was most comfortable to live? Give reasons for your answer.
8. Were ordinary people in either of these societies able to make their own choices about how they were governed?
9. Did the Celts in Britain have any more choice about how they were governed when the Romans took over?

LIVING IN THE COUNTRYSIDE

The majority of people in the Roman Empire lived in the countryside and not in towns. The best known archaeological remains from the countryside are the villas, large farmhouses at the centre of rich estates. In Britain over six hundred have been discovered but they can be found all over the Empire.

WHERE THE PEOPLE LIVED

1 Look at source A. Where have most of the villas been found in Britain?
2 Compare source A with source B. Explain whether you think that the villas shown on the map were the only farms in the country?

Clearly there were other kinds of farm in Roman Britain besides the villas. To investigate life in the countryside you will need information about all types of farm, not just those built by the rich. The first question this chapter will investigate is:

∾ *Did the Romans change the way of life in the countryside or did it stay the same over a long period of time?*

Source A
Map showing the distribution of villas in Britain.

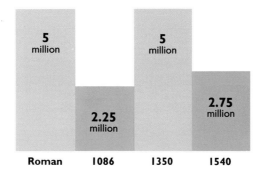

5 million		5 million	
	2.25 million		2.75 million
Roman	1086	1350	1540

Source B
The population of Britain.

CHANGES: LIFE IN THE COUNTRYSIDE

Look carefully at the sources on pages 16 and 17.
1 What do sources G and I tell us about farming from the Iron Age to the Saxon period?
2 Do the sources D, F and H tell the same story? Write down the two main points that are being made in these sources.
3 Source K shows the settlements in one area during the three different periods.
    a It shows there were many farms in this valley in the Iron Age. Describe how this agrees or disagrees with source G.
    b What sort of increase or change in the number of farms is shown in the Roman period?
    c What features appear in the Anglo-Saxon period that cannot be found in the other two?
4 Did the countryside change during the Roman period, or was it much the same throughout the Iron Age, the Roman period and into Anglo-Saxon times? Give evidence to support your answer.

Source C

Irregularly shaped 'Celtic fields' at Fyfield Down, Wiltshire

Source D

By the end of the Iron Age nearly the whole of England was being farmed, with a large population living in a wide variety of settlements, and occupying all kinds of soils and positions.

(C. Taylor, *Village and Farmstead*, 1983)

Source E

A Roman farm at Clay Lane, Northamptonshire.

Living in the countryside before the Romans arrived

Living in the countryside during the Roman period

Source F

By the Fourth Century AD England had a very large population, with tens of thousands of settlements ranging from single farms to hamlets and villages. Every available area of suitable land was being farmed.

(C. Taylor, *Village and Farmstead*, 1983)

Source G

Most British farms were on the hills where the soil was light and easy to plough. Lower down, near the valleys, the Romans set up farms of their own, which were later copied by the British farmers. These farms were called villas.

(J. Patrick and M. Packham, *Age of Invasions*, 1985)

Life in the countryside after the Romans

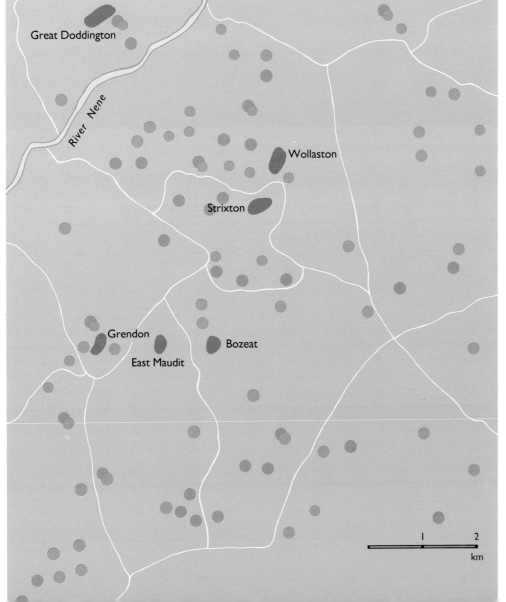

Source H

A reconstruction of an Anglo-Saxon village at West Stow, Suffolk.

Source I

The Saxons came not to a new and relatively untouched country but to a very old one, a country where most of the best places had been occupied not once but many times by a variety of people living in a great variety of settlements.

(C. Taylor, *Village and Farmstead*, 1983)

Source J

The Anglo-Saxons were skilled farmers. When they landed in Britain they took over land that had been cultivated in Roman times, but more often cleared areas of woodland by burning down the trees.

(J. Patrick and M. Packham, *Age of Invasions*, 1985)

Source K

Iron Age, Roman and Anglo-Saxon settlements in the valley of the River Nene, Northamptonshire.

Iron Age settlement
Roman settlement
Anglo-Saxon village
Parish boundary

What was a villa?

The Roman word villa means farm. This is the definition that was used by the Romans who built the villas. However, archaeologists today think that a villa was more than just a farm. Some archaeologists think that villas were big country houses. Others believe that many villas were at the centre of large farming estates with lots of smaller farms surrounding them.

Here are a range of sources that tell us about villas in the Empire, and help us answer this chapter's second main question:

How comfortable was the way of life for people who lived in the countryside?

Source L

A reconstruction of a large villa at Littlecote.

Source M

A Roman wallpainting of a villa from Trier.

Source N

A Roman mosaic from Tabarka in Tunisia showing a villa.

Source O

You may wonder at why my villa is such a joy to me, but once you realise the attractions of the house itself, its position and its extensive sea-front, you will have your answer.

(Pliny, a Roman writer and senator, writing about AD 100)

Source P

A farm should be in an area with a healthy climate, with fertile soil. The villa should have three sections: the villa urbana – the house of the owner, the villa rustica – the house of the farm manager and workers and the villa fructuaria – the storehouse. The villa urbana should have both winter and summer rooms. The baths should face the setting of the sun in the summer to keep them lighted from midday to evening.

(Lucius Columella, *On Agriculture*, AD 60)

Source Q

A plan of Bignor villa, West Sussex.

M — Mosaic floor
T — Tessellated floor
H — Hypocaust

^N

private courtyard or garden

baths

oxen (plough-teams)

farmyard

aisled barn

EVIDENCE: WHAT WAS A VILLA?

1 What do sources N and P tell us about Roman villas?
2 Use sources L–Q. Was life comfortable in a Roman villa?
3 Which of these sources are most useful for investigating:
   decoration in villas?
   the number of rooms in villas?
   where villas were built?
4 Are the written sources more valuable than the pictorial sources as evidence for life in villas? Explain your answer.
5 Source L shows a painted reconstruction of a villa at Littlecote. How reliable is this source to an historian trying to find out about life in the Roman Empire?
6 What sort of people lived in these buildings? Were they wealthy or poor? Write down the evidence to back-up your statements.

You now have a good idea of what a Roman villa was like. Remembering the work you did on the social structure of the Empire you must now apply what you learnt to your hypothesis and consider whether additions need to be made to it.

'Living in the countryside could be comfortable but it depended on . . .'

TRAVEL AND TRADE

📜 What was it like travelling in the Roman Empire?

How did you get to school today? No doubt your journey was mainly by road. As you came to school you probably passed a great variety of travellers, such as farmers and businessmen, who need a good road system. Some of the travellers, like yourself, were making a local trip. Others were on part of a long journey, perhaps carrying things to sell. The Romans relied on the roads in exactly the same way. This chapter will investigate the question:

∽ Did the roads make life more comfortable for the people in the Roman Empire?

Source A

A reconstruction of the Forum, the centre of Roman Wroxeter.

The Roman army built roads in a newly conquered area to make sure that the countryside remained under their control. They built a road system that allowed soldiers to move quickly to any problem area. For example, in the first four years after the Emperor Claudius invaded Britain, the army built over one thousand miles of road without any machinery.

Once an area was under the control of the army, new towns and settlements would be built. A good road system was very important. The towns needed good roads for trade and the government needed the roads to keep in touch with the different parts of the Empire. In the Second Century AD,

Suetonius described how Augustus introduced the imperial post that carried messages to all parts of the Empire:

'At the beginning of his reign he kept in close touch with affairs in the Empire by relays of runners stretched out at short intervals along the highways; later he organised a chariot service, based on posting stations —

which has proved satisfactory.'

Local roads were also important. The towns were sometimes slow to grow but even if they did not have many people they still needed to have good reliable supplies of food. It was the villa estates that provided much of this food and it was delivered by road or by water transport.

📖 How were the roads built?

Source B

First there's the job of marking a furrow, opening up a track and excavating a trench.

Next the trench must be refilled with material packed down as a foundation for the surface of the road: the ground must not give way when the stone slabs are laid. When they have been laid, they are held in place with kerb stones. Look at the gang of men at work!

Some are busy felling trees and clearing hillsides: others are cutting and smoothing rocks and planing huge wooden beams, while stonemasons cement the stones together. Others work hard to divert the course of streams and pump out water that fills the trenches. The countryside and the woods all around are filled with noise and the sound of workmen.

(Statius. From his poems written in the First Century AD)

Source C

Cross-section of a Roman road

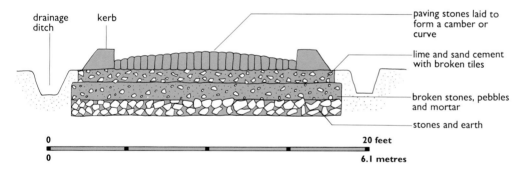

drainage ditch — kerb — paving stones laid to form a camber or curve — lime and sand cement with broken tiles — broken stones, pebbles and mortar — stones and earth

0 — 20 feet
0 — 6.1 metres

Source D

There are also local roads that branch off from the main highway and lead to other public ways. They are built and maintained by local landowners who have the job of looking after the stretch of road going over their land. Anyone can travel along all these public ways.

Finally, there are the ways leading across private estates that can be used by everyone who needs to reach their fields. These ways lead off local roads. The public highways, the local roads and the private ways were laid out to make travelling easier.

(Siculus Flaccus. A Roman surveyor of the First Century AD)

Source E
A Roman road.

ROMAN ROADS

1 How many different types of road were there in Roman times?
2 Why did the Roman army build so many roads?
3 Who used the different types of roads?
4 How would an historian find out how much the different roads were used?
5 How were local roads kept in good condition?
6 Write a paragraph describing the building of a Roman road. Use the sources as the basis of your description.

🎌 How did people travel?

Source F

In Roman times people travelled a great deal, walking and riding on horseback or in (horse-drawn) vehicles. Very long journeys were made on foot. The horse and the mule were used as steeds or as pack animals. They wore light shoes, rather than ordinary horse-shoes and in preference to the hard road, kept to the sandy tracks alongside.

(Raymond Chevallier, *Roman Roads*, 1976)

Source G

From London to Dover Port. 68¾ miles
From London to Rochester. 28¾ miles
From Rochester to Canterbury. 25½ miles
From Canterbury to Dover Port. 14½ miles

(Part of the Second Century AD Antonine Itinerary – a Roman travel guide)

Source H

A horse drawn vehicle.

Source I

A map of the main roads in Roman Britain

TRAVEL IN THE ROMAN EMPIRE

1 What methods of travel were used by the Romans?
2 What sources of power were used to transport people and goods in Roman times?
3 What items would a wealthy Roman have used to plan a long journey?
4 Describe the benefits of travelling by water rather than by road?
5 Explain whether all people travelled in the same way regardless of their wealth?
6 After the Roman Empire, new sources of power were introduced to make travel and transport easier. Draw a time line showing when these changes were introduced. You will need to use other books to help you answer this question.

Source K

The lazy boatman lets the mule graze; he ties a rope to a stone and lies on his back snoring. When the day dawns we realize that the barge is making no progress. This is remedied when a furious passenger jumps ashore, seizes a branch of willow and wallops the mule and the boatman on the head and back.

(Horace, writing of his travels in about 38 BC)

⚜ What did people buy and sell in the Empire?

Source L
Roman power has brought the world together. Is there anything more wonderful than to witness this never-ending exchange between different parts of the world.

(From a letter by Pliny the Elder, First Century AD)

Source M
Around the Mediterranean are many countries sending an endless stream of goods into Rome. To Rome is transported by land and sea whatever is produced. What you cannot see in Rome does not exist.

(Aelius Aristides, *To Rome*, written in the First Century AD)

Pliny the Elder had no doubt about the value of good roads and communications across the empire. He thought that the Romans had created a peaceful empire. It was the army who kept the peace and guaranteed that traders and travellers could move about freely.

Goods could be transported over long distances without the risk of them being stolen by bandits. This created a chance to trade in any country in the empire. In the First Century BC Strabo the Greek geographer described how 'a large amount of tin coming from Britain finds its way over to the shores of Gaul (France). Through Gaul the traders take it by pack-horse to the people of Marseilles.'

Another major advantage was that a single currency was used throughout the empire. The same coins were used in Syria in the east as were to be found in Britain in the west. This made it much easier for foreign merchants to buy and sell their goods. It is only in the 1990's that we are getting close to returning to this situation once again!

What trade goods did people buy and sell in the Empire?

Today we are used to buying goods made in factories in different parts of the world. In Roman times the only thing that was made in large quantities and then widely distributed was pottery. Nearly everything else was made locally by craftsmen who could produce most things that the average household might need, so long as they had the raw materials. It was the trade in these raw materials and in food that dominated trade in the Roman Empire.

The most important area for trade was the Mediterranean Sea. It was cheaper and quicker to transport bulky raw materials and foodstuffs by water. The rivers that ran into the Mediterranean and the sea itself were used rather than the much slower land routes.

Rome, with a population of one million people was the biggest market for food and for the expensive luxury goods that only the wealthy could buy.

The armies on the frontiers of the Empire provided farmers with a market for their produce. Vast

Source N

Map of trade in the Roman Empire.

BRITAIN
- TIN (FROM CORNWALL)
- LEAD
- SLAVES
- WOOL HIDES

GERMANY
- TIMBER
- SOAP
- SLAVES
- HAIR (FOR WIGS)

GREECE, GREEK ISLANDS & TURKEY
- WORKS OF ART
- OLIVE OIL
- SLAVES
- HONEY
- TIMBER
- MARBLE
- HORSES
- POTTERY

FRANCE
- BUILDING STONE
- POTTERY
- TEXTILES
- METALS

BLACK SEA AREA OF TURKEY
- FISH
- TIMBER
- WOOL
- HEMP
- PITCH

SPAIN
- GRAIN
- OLIVE OIL
- WINE
- WAX
- SALT
- SILVER
- HORSES

ARABIA & THE INDIAN/CHINA TRADE ROUTE
- COTTON
- CHINESE SILK
- JEWELLERY
- PERFUMES
- SPICES

AFRICA
- IRON

EGYPT & NORTH AFRICA
- GRAIN
- FIGS
- PAPYRUS (FOR PAPER)
- DYES (FOR CLOTHES)
- DATES

EGYPT
- WILD ANIMALS (FOR AMPHITHEATRE)

0   500 MILES
    800 KM

amounts of wheat, oil and other supplies were moved to feed them.

Every area also produced food and other items for the local population. These were sold in towns, villages or beside the busy main roads. Some parts of the Empire specialized in certain types of goods that could not be found elsewhere. These goods would get a higher price and it would be worth transporting them long distances. Britain exported wool and woollen cloaks that looked very similar to a modern duffle coat. Other exports included tin, gold, lead, animals, hides and wheat. Imports included luxury goods like glass, wine, fine pottery and jewellery that were not made in Britain.

By the Third Century AD, Britain, like many of the other provinces, had started to produce its own luxury goods such as leather, glass, textiles, wood and metal. Many of these items have been found by archaeologists. Unfortunately, the most common trade goods like food and raw materials are rarely found because they do not survive like metals and pottery.

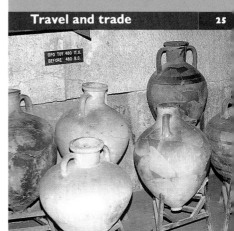

Source O
Roman amphorae used to transport and store such things as wine, oil and fish paste.

Source P
The wreck of a Roman cargo ship carrying sarcophagi.

A ROMAN SHIPWRECK

1 How did the divers who discovered this wreck know that it was a Roman ship?
2 What was the ship carrying?
3 Why has very little of the ship survived?
4 What do the remains of a Roman ship like this tell the historian about the Roman Empire?
5 Aristides in source M seems to be exaggerating the importance of Rome. Does this mean that the source is:
   a useless
   b very useful
   c sometimes useful, sometimes not useful.
   Explain your answer.
6 Why were the people in Britain able to buy goods that had been made in countries at the other end of the Roman Empire?
7 What sort of people were able to own and use luxury goods?
8 Did ordinary people in Britain benefit from the trade with the rest of the Empire?
9 Do you think that Roman roads and transport helped to make life more comfortable for the people of the Empire?

LIVING IN THE TOWNS

Source A
Pompeii.

Source B
A plan of the Roman town of Silchester.

When archaeologists uncovered the remains of the Roman town of Pompeii it gave us a very good idea of life in a town in the Roman Empire. There are other towns, mainly in desert regions, that have survived. However, none of them contain all the everyday objects that were buried when the volcanic ash covered Pompeii. Examining these towns can give us some clues about what other towns in the Empire looked like.

Around the Mediterranean towns and cities had been built for many years before the Roman Empire began. During the Roman Empire these towns were rebuilt and many of them had the same street pattern and buildings.

In Britain there were no towns with paved streets and brick buildings before the Romans invaded in AD 43. There were some very large British settlements but these were not organised like the Roman towns that replaced them. Towns like Canterbury were completely new.

In this chapter you will be focussing on the question:

∞ *What was it like living in the towns of the Roman Empire?*

Using a table like the one on the right will help you concentrate on the question as you look at different aspects of town life. You could work in groups with different groups tackling different topics.

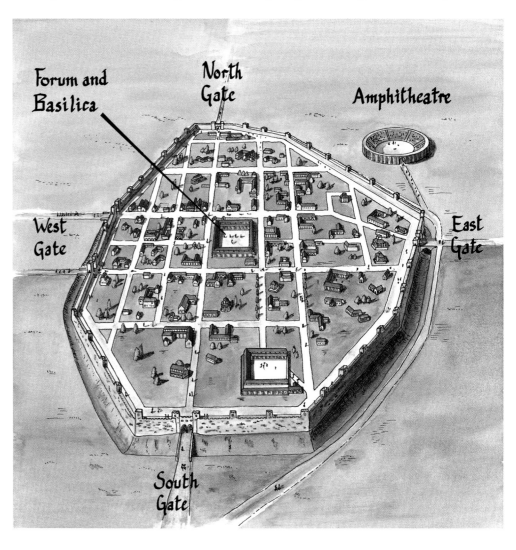

Forum and Basilica

North Gate

Amphitheatre

West Gate

East Gate

South Gate

	Was life the same for everyone?	Evidence to support answer	Types of source available
Public Health			
Medicine			
Beliefs/Religion			
Clothing			
Entertainment			

Source A gives you an idea of what Roman towns looked like. These towns are now ruins, but when an artist draws a reconstruction we can see more clearly what the towns would have looked like.

Artists who produce these reconstructions use their imaginations but more importantly they base their drawings on the evidence they have collected.

The reconstructions of Silchester and Canterbury show us what a Roman town looked like. It was surrounded by a town wall with strong gates. In the centre was a public area called the forum. The most important temples and the buildings where the town council met were here. The theatre was used for entertainments such as plays.

A reconstruction of Roman Canterbury c. AD 300.

ROMAN TOWNS

1 Describe the street pattern in Silchester. What does this tell you about the building of the town?
2 How many different kinds of house can you see in Canterbury?
3 Do you think the houses were lived in by the rich or the poor?
4 How many different types of transport can you see being used?
5 What building materials were used?
6 What kind of roofing was used on the buildings?
7 How did the townspeople use their leisure time?
8 Why do you think the local British people went to live in these new towns?
9 Silchester has strong walls and gates. What does this tell you about the history of the town?

How healthy was life in the towns?

Public health in Rome

The population of Rome and many of the other great cities in the Empire enjoyed the use of huge public baths. In Rome the baths were open to anyone who could pay one quadrans, the smallest Roman coin. Often entry was free. The baths in Rome were very large buildings. St Paul's Cathedral in London covers an area of about 6,000 square metres. But the Baths of Carcalla in Rome covered 25,000 square metres, and they were smaller than the Baths of Diocletian which could accommodate over 3,000 people at a time.

In AD 50 the population of Rome was about one million. You can imagine the amount of water that was needed by each person for drinking, cooking, washing and for getting rid of the sewage and waste. Add to this the demands of the big public baths and the public fountains, and you can see that the supply of water and the disposal of sewage needed to be well organized.

Source C
A plan of the public baths in Rome.

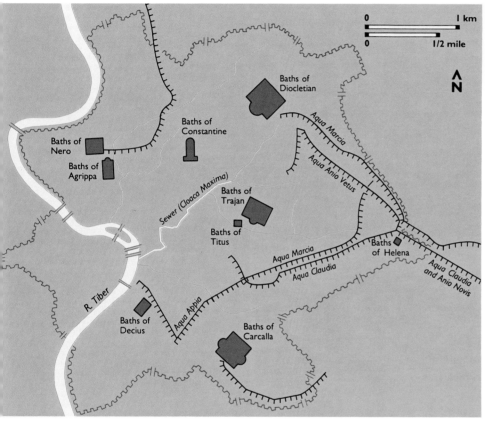

Source D
The water commissioners shall make sure that the public fountains bring water continuously for the use of the people day and night.

(A law passed by the Senate in 11 BC)

Source E
Who used the water in Rome?

The Emperor	17.1%
Industry and the houses of the rich	38.6%
The Government buildings	24.1%
The Army	2.9%
The Public baths	3.9%
Public fountains and tanks	13.4%

Source F
My job is concerned with the comfort and the health of Rome. The results of the great number of reservoirs, buildings, fountains and water basins can be seen in the improved health of Rome. The city looks cleaner, and the causes of the unhealthy air which gave Rome a bad name are now removed. Compare such important engineering works with the useless pyramids!

(Sextus Frontius, who was responsible for the water and drainage in Rome between AD 97–104)

Source G
The old men still admire the city sewers, the greatest achievement of all. They were built 700 years ago and they are still undamaged. When Agrippa took charge of the sewers he travelled on a tour of inspection under the city in a boat. There are seven rivers made to flow in seven tunnels under the city. They finally run into one great sewer.

(Pliny, Natural History, AD 50)

Source H

The Marcian canal roars past my room and yet there's not a drop of water in the house.

(Martial, *Epigrams*, First Century AD)

Source I

We think ourselves poor if our walls are not covered with huge mirrors and our swimming pools lined with marble, and if the water does not pour from silver spouts! And I am talking only about the baths of the common people.

(Seneca, writing in the First Century AD)

Source J

Along your way each open window may be a death trap. So hope and pray, poor man, that the housewives drop nothing worse on your head than a bedpan full of slops.

(Juvenal, *Satires*, Second Century AD)

Source K

Roman Lincoln had an efficient sewerage system, the main sewer running beneath the main road and consisting of a stone walled and slab roofed tunnel up to 1.5 m high and 1.2 m wide.

(R. Muir, *Portraits of the Past*, 1988)

Source L

Supplying Rome with water.

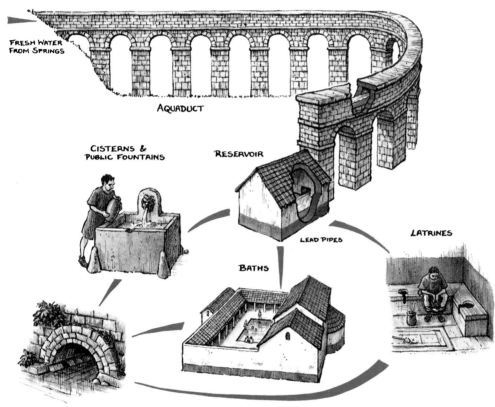

FRESH WATER FROM SPRINGS

AQUADUCT

CISTERNS & PUBLIC FOUNTAINS

RESERVOIR

LEAD PIPES

LATRINES

BATHS

SEWERS EMPTYING INTO RIVER TIBER

Source M

The Cloaca Maxima, one of Rome's main sewers.

EVIDENCE: PUBLIC HEALTH IN THE ROMAN EMPIRE

1 Read source F. Why did the Romans think it was so important to have a good supply of clean water?
2 Read sources D, F and H. Which of these sources is most useful for investigating the effectiveness of the water supply?
3 Was everyone in Rome well supplied with water? Use the sources to support your answer.
4 Read sources H and J. Do their comments mean that the other sources cannot be believed and are of no use to an historian?
5 Did every town and village in the Empire have the same sort of system of public health?
6 Complete your grid like the one on page 27. How does the investigation of public health affect your ideas about what it was like to live in the Roman Empire?

🖹 What was it like in the Roman Empire if you were ill?

Many of the ideas and methods used by Roman doctors were based on those of the Greeks. The Greeks believed in the healing power of the gods but they also carefully observed the causes and cures of illnesses.

Following the example of the Greeks, the Romans also observed the causes of illness and had a variety of cures. They prayed to the Gods who they thought could cure those who were ill. They made sacrifices and presented gifts to the Gods. Source N shows one such offering.

Other forms of superstition led the Romans to use unusual methods and potions to try to cure themselves.

Source O

A quick cure for broken bones is to apply the ashes of the jawbone of a pig. For fractured ribs use goat's dung mixed with old wine.

(Pliny the Elder, *Natural History*, First Century AD)

Source P

White of egg can help heal wounds. The yolk of an egg hard boiled in vinegar and roasted with pepper stops diarrhoea. Nits can be removed with dog fat.

(Pliny the Elder, *Natural History*, First Century AD)

'Health begins the moment a man wakes up'. Like many people today the Roman doctors encouraged a healthy life with exercise, good food and hygiene. Sport was encouraged as a way of keeping fit. The great baths in the big cities were not just for bathing and keeping clean, they were places where men and women could go for exercise, a massage or sporting activities.

The most famous doctor during the Roman period was a Greek called Claudius Galen. He believed, like earlier Greek doctors, that the body was made up of four humours or fluids: blood, phlegm, yellow bile and black bile.

Source N

What problem did the owner of this offering suffer from?

Source Q

The Action plan

1 Exercise regularly.
2 Get moving – choose activities you enjoy.
3 Watch your weight and stay slim.
4 Reduce the fatty foods you eat.
5 Eat more fibre – wholemeal bread, fruit, vegetables cereals and potatoes.

(Healthy living advert 1991)

Source R

When all these humours are truly balanced a person feels in the most perfect health. Illness happens when there is too much of one humour or too little.

(Hippocrates, A Greek doctor born in 406 BC)

Galen found out a little about how the body works by dissecting the bodies of animals and humans. Combining this with some ideas from India and many common-sense remedies he wrote down all this information which became the most popular medical text-book for well over the next twelve hundred years.

Source S

The medical ideas of doctors like Galen probably had little effect on the ordinary people. Only a few of the richer Romans could afford a doctor. Most people were still peasant farmers and lived in the country villages where there were no doctors. Medical care was still a matter for the family as it had always been.

(J. Scott, *Medicine Through Time*, 1987)

Source T

Oh those terrible discussions at the bedside of the patient, no doctor agreeing with another. Hence the gloomy words on some tombstones: *it was the crowd of doctors that killed me.*

(Pliny, a Roman writer and Senator, writing about AD 100)

Source U

Skilled Roman doctors could not save people from the illnesses that today can be cured by a course of antibiotics or a few days in hospital. Appendicitis, for example, today removed by a routine operation, was always fatal. Romans had some quite effective drugs but no anaesthetics. Surgery was terrifying, agonizing, and dangerous.

(Simon James, author of the book *Ancient Rome*, 1990)

Source W

A soldier who is on duty in the cold without the proper clothing is not in a state to have good health or to march. He must not drink water from marshes. Daily exercise say the generals is better than the doctor for the soldiers. If during the summer or the autumn a group of soldiers stays too long in one place they begin to suffer from the effects of polluted water, and are made miserable by the smell of their own excrement. The air becomes unhealthy and they catch diseases. They should avoid this by marching to a new camp.

(Vegetius, *A Military Digest*, Fourth Century AD)

Source V
Modern operating theatre.

Source X
Modern faith healer.

PEOPLE IN THE PAST: ROMAN MEDICINE

1 In what ways was Roman medical care similar to medical care today?
2 In what ways was Roman medical care different to medical care today?
3 How were Roman medical treatments connected with:
   a religion?
   b Public health?

4 a What ideas did Romans have about how to stay healthy and treat disease?
   b Why were some people's ideas different from others?
5 Now fill in your grid like the one on page 27. What was it like in the Roman Empire if you were ill?

Source C

Jupiter, King of the Gods.

What religions did people believe in?

In the very early years of the Republic the people who lived in and near Rome believed in spirits. They felt that the spirits would look after them so long as sacrifices were made to keep the spirits happy. 'The Romans looked after the spirits and the spirits looked after the Romans.'

Source A

When the new owner arrives at the farm he should go round the farm as soon as he has paid his respects to the spirits of the house.

(Cato, *On Agriculture*, written in the Second Century BC)

There was not just one spirit but many. For example, if you wanted to keep your oxen in good health you would sacrifice to Mars Silvanus, god of agriculture. If it was your own health that you were concerned with you would make a sacrifice to the goddess Hygeia. The Romans worshipped their Gods and made sacrifices to them, either at home in private shrines, or in public at the great temples.

Source B

A procession and sacrifice

In the home the shrines were very small. Source D is a good example of the sort of shrine that was kept for the household spirits. A shrine such as this might be for Janus, the spirit of doorways, who kept families from harm. Throughout their lives the Romans looked to these spirits for help and protection through the prayers and sacrifices by the male head of the household, the paterfamilias (the latin word pater means father).

In about 300 BC the Romans began to worship the Greek Gods.

They still believed in their old spirits but they gave the Greek gods new names and made them part of their own religion. For example the Greek gods Zeus and Athene became the Roman gods Jupiter and Diana.

These gods were worshipped in public places in temples similar to those of the Greeks. They were often made up of a single room called the cella. This was surrounded by columns and entered up steps through a fine entrance called a portico. Source G shows what a temple looked like.

Source D

A First Century AD household shrine from Pompeii.

As the Empire grew, more new religions and gods were worshipped by the Romans and those who lived in the Empire. The Emperor Augustus was even made a god after his death. This began a tradition of making the Emperors gods. The law stated that as long as you offered prayers to the Roman gods and the Emperor you could worship your own spirits in your own way.

However a new religion from the East, Christianity, had believers who refused to pray to any god other than their own. This led to the Christians breaking the law and sometimes being badly treated. Like many other religions in the Second Century, Christianity spread rapidly. The churches became better organised and several of the 'fathers' of the church were popular writers and thinkers. Gradually more people joined Christian churches and the leaders, who were often important people, spread the ideas of Christianity throughout the empire.

Source E

But no matter how hard he tried, the Emperor Nero could not stop people thinking that he had started the great fire in Rome in AD 64. To stop the gossip he blamed the Christians who were already hated for their religion. Nero punished them with the worst tortures and cruelty he could think up.

(Tacitus, *Annals*, Second Century AD)

Source F

By the end of the Third Century, about a tenth of the population of the empire may already have been Christian, one emperor had been, and another seems to have included Jesus Christ among the gods honoured privately in his household.

(J. Roberts, *The World of Greece and Rome*, 1980)

It was in AD 395 that Christianity was made the official religion of the Roman Empire. From this time Christianity grew to become one of the great world religions.

Source G

The Maison Carree in Nîmes, France. A Roman temple built in about 19 BC

PEOPLE IN THE PAST: RELIGION AND BELIEFS

1   Why do you think that the Romans had gods for the sun, the sea and the many things that were part of their lives?

2   The Romans allowed people in the Empire to worship their own gods as long as they worshipped the Emperor. Why do you think that they insisted that the Emperor should be worshipped?

3   Why were the early Christians persecuted?

4   Why do you think many poor people became Christians?

5   How did the existence of the Roman Empire help the spread of Christianity and other religions?

6   Now fill in your grid. Do you think that Roman attitudes to religion helped improve the lives of people in the empire?

Source H

Fish, the secret symbol of the early Christians. The Greek word for fish includes the initials of Jesus Christ. IXTHUS .

📖 What was clothing and fashion like in the Roman Empire?

Source I

There is nothing worse than a woman with too much money. Her face – well what a sight! It's laughable. It's swollen with bread poultices and smells of sticky cream. Her husband's lips are glued to hers when he tries to give her a kiss.

(Juvenal, *Satires*, Second Century AD)

Source J

Galla, you live at home alright but not your beauty, that has travelled from the chemist's shop. Well, take your hair, that's made in Germany; at night you put your teeth away just like your dresses. When you get into bed the rest of you is boxed up in a hundred little boxes, even your face sleeps in a different place.

(Martial, *Epigrams*, First Century AD)

Source K

Fabella swears that she wears her own hair. Well Paulus, you're her boy-friend, is she telling lies?

Thais has black teeth. Laecania's are white. Do you know why? Laecania bought hers and Thais has her own.

(Martial, *Epigrams*, First Century AD)

Source L

In winter Augustus wore no fewer than four tunics and a heavy woollen cloak over his undershirt. Under that he wore a woollen vest as well as underpants and woollen socks.

(Suetonius, *Life of Augustus*, Second Century AD)

There are very few detailed descriptions like these of Roman clothing and fashion. The best sources of information are from paintings, mosaics and sculptures.

Source M

A painting of a Roman woman wearing make-up.

Source N

Two hairstyles fashionable during the Roman Empire.

Source O

Women wore a colourful dress called a stola. Make-up, jewellery and different hairstyles went in and out of fashion much as they do today.

Source P

Roman citizens were allowed to wear a toga. The toga was the equivalent of a modern suit, a standard form of dress for the well off. Usually white and made of wool, it was worn over a tunic and a loin cloth that was tied around the waist.

Source Q
The Emperor Trajan gives food to the needy in AD 114.

Source R
Men usually wore a tunic.

Source S
Victorian and punk fashions.

Source T
Footwear was mainly in the style of sandals, made from leather with strong soles.

EVIDENCE: CLOTHES AND FASHION IN THE ROMAN EMPIRE

1 Which sources do you think tell you most about Roman dress? Explain the choices that you made.

2 Do you think Sources I–K give reliable accounts of Roman fashions? Explain your answer.

3 **a** Put the pictures in source S in the right order. Explain how you were able to do this.
b Can you use the same technique to put the Roman hairstyles (source N) in order?

4 **a** What is the main difference between the two groups of people in source Q?
b Is it more useful to look at one group rather than the other when trying to find out about Roman fashions?

5 Now fill in your grid. Did everyone have the same standard of dress in the Roman Empire?

🖿 Entertainment in the Roman Empire

Rome and the larger Roman towns offered a range of entertainments. There were plays and music at the theatres but also horrifying blood sports where gladiators fought each other to the death, and events where animals were killed for people's amusement.

Source A
Mosaic of an animal fight.

What was it like being a Gladiator?

One unexpected type of evidence from Pompeii is graffiti. The walls of the amphitheatre and some town houses had slogans written on them. These mention some of the sporting heroes of Pompeii, particularly the gladiators.

Source B
Aemilius wrote this by the light of the moon
Celadus, glory and heart-throb of the girls
Actus of the Julian School has won fifty times
Quintus has gained his discharge after 33 fights
(Graffiti from a wall in Pompeii, AD 79)

Source C
Murranus of the Neronian school with three fights was killed.
    Cycnus of the Julian school with eight fights, won. Atticus from Greece with fourteen fights was pardoned.
(A results board from Pompeii, AD 79)

Source D
A vase from Colchester Museum. Appeal to the finger. To the left is Memnon a secutor and to the right a retiarius called Valentinus.

Gladiators were slaves, criminals or prisoners of war who were given the choice of execution or the chance of freedom by fighting successfully before the crowds. Occasionally women became gladiators. The Gladiators were trained in special schools but wore different types of armour and carried a variety of weapons. If they failed to fight with enthusiasm they might be flogged or scorched with red hot irons. They had no choice but to fight for their lives. Some gladiators were professional fighters and became famous, earning huge sums of money. The majority died in combat.

When a man was wounded he threw down his shield and raised the index finger of his left hand, asking for mercy. If the sponsor of the games, or the crowd, thought the man had fought well he might be spared. If not his opponent killed him. An official dressed as Charon, a demon, then clubbed the fallen gladiator to make sure he was dead. To the sound of trumpets the body was then dragged from the arena.

Source E
One day I went to the Midday Games, hoping to enjoy some light entertainment, rather than the usual bloodshed. It was the exact opposite; the other shows I had seen were a picnic in comparison. This was pure murder. When one man fell another would immediately take his place. And this went on and on, till none are left, even the last was killed. You may say but 'that one committed a robbery'. So what? Does he deserve to be crucified? 'He committed murder.' Even so does he deserve to die like this? What sort of punishment do you deserve for watching him? All day the crowd cries 'Kill him, flog him, burn him! Why does he run on the sword so timidly? Why is he so unwilling to die?'
(From the letters of Seneca, written in the First Century AD)

The Colosseum in Rome is the most famous amphitheatre built by the Romans. Holding about 50,000 spectators it provided entertainment in the form of the games which included gladiators, animal hunts and even sea fights on an artificial lake.

What were the other entertainments?

Not all Roman entertainments were as bloodthirsty as the fights between gladiators. Many large towns had theatres where plays and religious festivals took place. Some larger theatres in the Empire could seat an audience of over 9000. Comedies, tragedies and farces were very popular.

The actors performed on an open stage facing the audience, who were seated on tiers of seats. Admission to the plays was free, paid for by the wealthy politicians and merchants of the town. Actors and actresses were as popular then as they are now.

Source F

'Actius, darling of the people, come back quickly'
'Paris, pearl of the stage'.
(Graffiti from Pompeii, AD 79)

Even bigger crowds went to see the chariot races that were held in Rome's Circus Maximus, a large stadium about 600 metres long. Chariots drawn by two or four horses would race seven times around the central island. There were often accidents, especially at the turns and there was sometimes fighting in the crowd. Audiences of 250,000 packed into the Circus Maximus to see the charioteers.

Source G

Gaius Apuleius, Charioteer of the Reds, a Spaniard, aged 42 years, 7 months and 23 days. He drove his first chariot for the Whites in AD 122. He won his first victory with that team shortly after. His first victory with the Reds was in AD 131.

Grand Totals: he drove for 24 years, started 4,257 races and won 1,462 of them. In all he won a total of 35,863,120 sesterces.

(An inscription found in Rome)

Source H

The Colosseum, built in AD 80 and named after the thirty metre high statue of the Emperor Nero that stood nearby. The floor of the arena has been removed to show the cells and cages where the prisoners, gladiators and animals were kept.

DIFFERENT VIEWS: ROMAN ENTERTAINMENT

1 Which of these statements are FACTS and which are OPINIONS?
   a Romans watched blood sports.
   b All Roman people were bloodthirsty.
   c Roman sports were exciting.
   d Most gladiators were killed.
2 There are no sources here about entertainment in Roman Britain.
   a What kinds of entertainment do you think there were in Roman Britain?
   b Compare your answer with others in your class. Why are some answers different from yours?
3 Films often show the Romans as bloodthirsty people, whose only entertainments were fights and dangerous races. Explain whether that is an accurate view of Roman people.
4 'Roman sports were cruel.'
   'Roman sports were fair.'
   a Can you support each of these statements using the sources?
   b Why might historians have different views about the cruelty of Roman sports?
5 Now fill in your grid and explain whether the entertainments mentioned here made life more attractive and comfortable in the Roman Empire.

A SOLDIER IN THE ROMAN ARMY

The army played an important role throughout the period of the Empire. It conquered new lands and protected the people in the Empire. Sometimes it kept the peace and was a force for good. On other occasions it was mis-used by its generals who wanted to become emperor. Any study of the Empire needs to include an investigation into life in the army, because the success of the army had much to do with the strength of the Empire, why it grew and why it lasted so long.

During the Republic the part-time army was made-up of Roman citizens and led by generals who often fought each other for control of the government. The army of the Empire was led by the emperor and soldiers served for a fixed number of years and were recruited from all over the Empire. They would become either legionaries (if they were Roman citizens) or auxiliaries (if they were freedmen or allies of Rome).

Tiberius Claudius Maximus: Legionary

At the beginning of this book you looked at a soldier's tombstone. It had been found in Northern Greece. The soldier was Tiberius Claudius Maximus who served in the army for 30 years, from AD 84, under the Emperors Domitian and Trajan. The sources on pages 38–41 will help you work out some details of his lifestory. The sources have been collected from different parts of the Empire and although they do not all refer to Tiberius himself, they each help to reconstruct a picture of what it was like to be an ordinary soldier, a legionary, in the Roman army. As you read through these pages make a list of the reasons why you think the Roman army was so successful.

The recruit

Only Roman citizens could join as legionaries and Tiberius would have signed-on for 25 years. His tombstone tells us that he spent most of his life as a soldier in the cavalry but he would have joined as a legionary, a foot soldier.

When legionaries signed-on they were organised into groups of eight men, enough to fill a tent or a barrack room. Their officer was a centurion who was in charge of a century, ten of these tent groups. There were six centuries in a cohort and ten cohorts in a legion and if you work it all out, there were about 4800 men in a legion! Each of the legionaries was carefully trained as a soldier and every man had a special job, perhaps as an engineer, craftsman or builder. Many of the men who joined the army did so to learn a trade to use when they left.

Source B

[missing name] is my dear friend and a capable fellow. He has asked me my lord, to recommend him to you. I therefore ask you, my lord, to grant him whatever he asks. Through helping him you have put me in your debt.

(A letter of recommendation written about AD 100 and preserved in the mud at Vindolanda – a Roman fort in the North of England)

Source C

Anyone who takes a look at the organisation of the army will see that they have not conquered a huge empire by luck. Plans are made before any action and these are followed by the army. It is no wonder the Roman Empire stretches from Africa to the Rhine, from the Euphrates to the Atlantic.

(*The Jewish War*, written by Josephus, a Roman historian of the First Century AD)

Source A
A Roman legionary
He is wearing a cuirass (chest and back armour) made from overlapping leather-lined strips of iron; a kilt of strips of leather covered in iron and iron greaves to protect his legs.

Source D

An aerial photograph of the Roman fort of Ardoch in Scotland. Notice the defensive ditches and ramparts.

Building a camp

Source E

The camp is conveniently divided into quarters by streets; the central area contains the officers' quarters, with the general's headquarters right in the middle. It looks something like a city with its forum, the centre for craftsmen, and the offices where the tribunes and the centurions settle disputes of the men.

The outer wall and buildings inside it are completed amazingly quickly, because of the number and the skill of the workmen. If necessary a ditch 6 feet deep and 6 feet wide, is dug round the outside of the wall. The outside looks like a wall, with towers spaced at regular intervals. Between the towers they position various artillery weapons for firing stones and arrows. There are four gates built into the rampart that surrounds the camp, one on each side.

(Josephus, *The Jewish War*, written in the First Century AD)

Source F

Whether the legion was staying in one place for a night or for several months it always built a camp so that it would not be surprised at night. The Roman army did not fight its battles by staying in these camps. It always moved out into the open countryside to attack the enemy or to defend the camp.

(Josephus, *The Jewish War*, written in the First Century AD)

Source G

For building the trenches they find it useful to have pick-axes, shovels, baskets and other equipment always on hand.

(Vegetius, *A Military Digest*, Fourth Century AD.)

A section of Trajan's Column, early Second Century, showing the building of a fort.

Training

Source H

Every soldier is exercised everyday as if it were in time of war. This is the reason they stand up so well in battle and do not tire.

(Josephus, *The Jewish War*, written in the First Century AD)

Source I

The young soldier must be given frequent practice in carrying loads of up to 60 pounds while marching at the normal speed, because on difficult campaigns they will have to carry their rations as well as their weapons. This is not difficult if they get enough practice.

(Vegetius, *A Military Digest*, Fourth Century AD)

Source J

At the beginning of their training recruits must be taught the marching in step. For nothing is so important on the march or in the field as all the men keeping their marching ranks. They will only learn to march quickly and in time with continuous practice, and so in the summer months they must complete a march of twenty miles in 5 hours at normal marching speed. When they march at the faster speed they must cover a distance of 24 miles in the same time.

(Vegetius, *A Military Digest*, Fourth Century AD)

Source K

The early Romans made round wicker shields twice as heavy as those used in battle and gave recruits wooden sticks instead of swords, again double the normal weight. They practice using these at stakes morning and afternoon. A stake six feet high is fixed into the ground firmly. The recruit practices with his wooden shield and wooden stick against this, just as if he was fighting a real enemy. Sometimes he aims at the head or the face, sometimes he threatens the thighs, and sometimes tries to strike the knees and legs. He gives ground, attacks and assaults the stake with all the skill and energy needed in real fighting against a real enemy.

(Vegetius, *A Military Digest*, Fourth Century AD)

Source L

A centurion named Lucilius was killed by his troops at the start of the mutiny. This man had earned their hatred because of the punishments he handed out to his men. They nick-named him 'Cedo alteram' (or 'give me another') because every time he broke his vine-stick on a soldier's back he called for another.

(Tacitus, *Annals*, First Century AD)

Source M
Recruits practising with wooden weapons.

Tiberius in Action

Most of a Roman soldier's life was spent preparing to fight, though actual fighting was very rare. Julius Caesar led an army for fourteen years and only once fought a battle where two armies faced each other over an open battlefield.

In Dacia (modern Romania) Tiberius would have marched long distances and faced enemies fighting for their lives using huge two-handed swords. The battles were only part of the activities of the army. There was also the building and engineering work. The

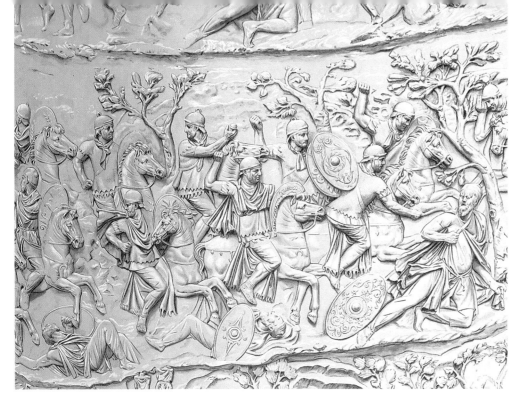

Trajan's Column was built in Rome to commemorate the victories of the Emperor in Dacia and tells the story of the campaign. This scene shows a cavalryman trying to stop Decebalus, the Dacian king, from killing himself.

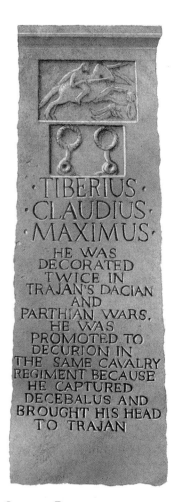

army constructed its own roads, bridges and any buildings that it might need, and all the work was done by the legionaries. On this campaign great bridges were built across the river Danube and roadways were constructed along the river gorge.

It was pure chance that led to the discovery of Tiberius' tombstone. From this we know something about an ordinary soldier and this information can be added to the scenes on Trajan's column, the only major surviving record of the campaign.

During his last years in the army, Tiberius fought with the Seventh Legion against the Parthians, who were attacking the eastern borders of the Empire in Mesopotamia, present day Iraq and Syria. In about AD 117 he was discharged from the army and returned to Northern Greece to retire.

Source O

Decebalus must have done everything he could to lose his pursuers. As long as there was the slightest hope, he pressed on. He was determined not to be taken, knowing that he would be flogged through the streets of Rome and ceremonially strangled. Finally, aware that the Roman cavalry were closing in, he dismounted, drew his dagger and cut his throat.

Tiberius saw the knife flash and dashed forward to grab the king's arm. But he was too late. Drawing his long sword he cut off the king's head and took it back to present to to the Emperor Trajan.

(Written by the archaeologist Peter Connolly in 1988)

Source P

Tiberius' Tombstone (see page 3). This is an extract from the tombstone in English.

EVIDENCE: TIBERIUS' TOMBSTONE AND TRAJAN'S COLUMN

1 What does Tiberius' tombstone tell you about the capture of Decebalus?
2 How reliable is Trajan's Column as a source, if you are trying to find out about the capture of Decebalus?
3 How much of the story by Peter Connolly can be backed-up by evidence from:
the tombstone of Tiberius?
Trajan's Column?
4 Write a description of what you think happened when Tiberius captured Decebalus. Remember, as historians, you must stick to using the sources as the basis of your story.
5 Why was it acceptable for Tiberius to cut off the head of Decebalus, yet today it would not be done even to an enemy?
6 'The Roman army helped to improve the lives of all the people in the Roman Empire.' Do you agree? Explain your answer?

THE FALL OF THE ROMAN EMPIRE

When did the Empire collapse?

Source A

In the West the Empire began to crack into pieces. Barbarian peoples began to move in and settle in parts of the Empire. Everything got mixed-up. New people were taking over, and after AD 476 nobody even pretended that there was an Emperor in Rome.

(T. Cairns, *The Romans and their Empire*, 1970)

Source B

The Western Empire was beginning to break-up under the strain of military defeat and economic crisis. The Rhine frontier was overrun in AD 406, and the German peoples poured into the Empire. In AD 410 Rome was sacked, and in AD 476 the last western emperor lost his power. Rome itself had fallen, but the Eastern Empire lived on.

The heavily populated and wealthy East also experienced wars, but it survived, until 1453. It still called itself 'Roman', but this Greek-speaking Christian state was very different from old Rome, and today is called the Byzantine Empire.

(Simon Jones, *Ancient Rome*, 1990)

Source C

The Empire was divided in AD 395 between two feeble sons Arcadius ruling the East and Honorius the West.

(D. Dudley, *Roman Society*, 1970)

Source F

A Map of the Eastern and Western Empires

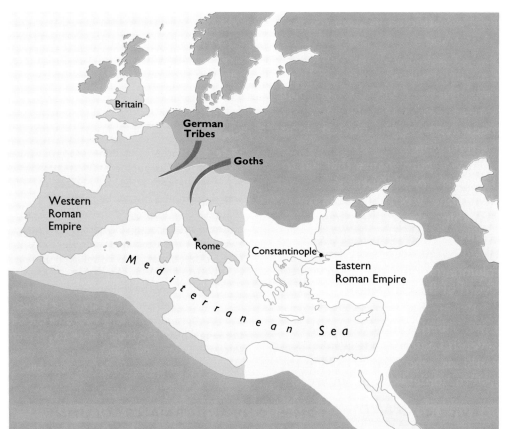

DIFFERENT VIEWS: THE END OF THE EMPIRE

1   Make a list of the historians and the dates when they say the Roman Empire ended and why they say it came to an end.
2   Historians disagree about when the Empire ended. Does this mean that one historian is right and the others are wrong? Explain your answer.
3   Why do you think that these historians have different explanations for the fall of the Roman Empire?

Source D

In the Fourth Century the Western Empire seized-up for lack of money. No new lands could be conquered to help pay for the defence of the Empire. As taxes went up, so more people moved into the countryside to avoid paying them. Less money meant a poorer army, and that meant paying barbarians to fight for the Empire.

(J. Roberts, *The World of Greece and Rome*, 1980)

Source E

The Goths found that their lances and horses could defeat the Roman army.

(Sir Charles Oman, *A Short History of the Byzantine Empire*, 1892)

It is not easy to say when the Roman Empire finally collapsed. We know that the Empire began in 27 BC when Augustus became Emperor and 'father of the fatherland', but deciding the date when the Empire came to an end is difficult. Just as the Romans conquered the Empire little by little then they also lost it bit by bit.

The Romans did not announce the end of the Empire. In most areas the main features of Roman life were replaced by the rule of the invading tribes. Sometimes these changes happened quickly, and on other occasions and in other places they were quite slow.

Historians can look back at these events (this is called hindsight) and decide when they think the Empire finally ended. The problem here is that historians do not always agree, they may use all the same sources and information to come to very different conclusions. They often decide that some events are more important than others. They pick dates and events that they think are significant. These events are, to them, the most important because they show that in their view a far-reaching change took place.

Roman soldiers leaving Britain in AD 415

A Turning Point?

This date (AD 415), like that of the invasion of Britain in AD 43, could be described as a turning point. A turning point is an event where things can be seen to change. After a turning point things are different.

A TURNING POINT IN HISTORY?

1 Did the Roman Empire end on the day that the soldiers left Britain?
2 Do you think that everything changed suddenly when the soldiers left, or did life carry on much the same as before?
3 Was AD 415 the beginning of a great change in what it was like to live in the areas that had once been the Roman Empire? Look back to page 8 for some evidence.
4 'What would it have been like living in the period after the fall of the Roman Empire?' How would you begin to investigate this question?

THE LEGACIES OF THE ROMAN EMPIRE

Most European cities, for example, Londinium - London, are built on top of a site chosen originally by the Romans.

The Roman Ideal.

The image of the power and success of the Empire and its Emperors has been copied by rulers up to the present day.

In the 4th. Century a Christian monk set down the Calendar we still use today

Language.

Wine – vinum
cheese – Caesus
street – strata

The Roman language, **Latin**, is the basis of many words in English. It is also the root of Italian, French, Spanish and Portuguese.

THE WESTERN EMPIRE.

The Holy Roman Empire.

Many kings and Emperors tried to rebuild the Roman Empire between **800** and the **20C** but none of them ruled an area as large as the Roman Empire of **117** A.D.

HAPSBURG EMPERORS 1273-1918

CHARLEMAGNE **800** A.D.

From the 1500's other Christian Churches.

The Renaissance.

An attempt in the 15th. and 16th. C. to find and copy the great achievements of the Roman Empire.

The Roman Catholic Church

509 B.C.	BC	AD		1000	1453
ROMAN REPUBLIC	ROMAN EMPIRE	500 AD.	EASTERN EMPIRE	BYZANTINE EMPIRE	

Pantheon.

St. Pauls

Docklands

An Architectural Heritage of Greek and Roman features has been used in the design of buildings. In the last **100** years it has come back into fashion again.

The Eastern Empire became the Byzantine Empire which lasted until it was destroyed by the Turks in **1453** A.D.

The Greek Orthodox Church.

THE EASTERN EMPIRE.

The Romans passed on Greek learning, Architecture and mathematics.

The Law.

measurement.   Medicine.

The Romans measured distances in feet and miles. The £ sign comes from the Latin 'libra' meaning one pound in weight.

many European countries have based their legal systems on the way the Romans did things

Learning

many of the Roman texts were copied into Greek in the Eastern Empire. They were copied back into Latin in the 15th. century.

and through the church reading and writing.

GALEN

LIVY

VIRGIL

TACITUS

1500   2000

The fall of the Roman Empire, its legacies and consequences

The world we live in today is linked to the past. It is the result of events and the things people did many years ago. Some of the features of today's life can be traced back to the Roman Empire. These features are sometimes described as the legacy of the Roman Empire.

Historians often separate the results of events, like the end of the Roman Empire, into short term consequences and long term consequences.

The short term consequences

The Roman Empire lasted for hundreds of years, but in the west it collapsed in the Fifth Century. The changes meant that for many, life was no longer as comfortable. A number of the towns in Britain were deserted, there was less trading between the different parts of the Empire and the Roman army no longer kept the peace. Things seemed to get worse instead of better.

The long term consequences

Although the Empire collapsed, many of the ideas and skills of its peoples have survived until today. For example, Christianity was the official religion of the Empire during its last years. When the Empire collapsed the barbarian kings, who were unable to read or write, destroyed the well organized Roman government. Only the Church kept alive the skills of reading and writing, because Christianity is a religion based on the written word, the Bible. If the Church had not kept these skills then the Church would have been very different and our language and the history of Europe might have been another story.

CAUSES AND CONSEQUENCES: THE LEGACIES OF THE EMPIRE

1 Why did the Roman Empire end?
2 Write two paragraphs, one describing the short term consequences of the collapse of the Roman Empire and a second describing the long term consequences. Use the information on pages 44 and 45 to help you.
3 a In your opinion which is the most important legacy of the Roman Empire?
  b Why might other people make a different choice?
4 Did changes in the past result in life after the end of the Roman Empire getting:
  a better
  b worse
  c a mixture of both
  Explain your answer.
5 Why do you think that Roman ideas have been copied in so many ways?
6 How have the Romans influenced the way you live today? To answer this question you will need to look carefully at pages 44 and 45.

WHAT WAS IT LIKE TO LIVE IN THE ROMAN EMPIRE?

At the beginning of this book you were asked to answer the question above. Your answer was based, at first, on what you already knew about the Roman Empire and the conclusions you could draw from the first few pages of sources.

Because the answer looked as if it might be quite complicated it was helpful to put the ideas together in the form of an hypothesis. Next, you were asked to investigate the question in greater detail and look at more evidence of life in the Roman Empire. The great advantage of this was that you were able to change your hypothesis as you examined new evidence. You will have discovered that there is no simple answer to our question. More often than not any answer has to include the phrase 'it depends on . . .' For example, life in a Roman villa could be very comfortable but it would depend very much whether you were the owner or a slave!

The historian's judgement is always based on the evidence.

CONCLUSIONS: LIFE IN THE ROMAN EMPIRE

1 Now that you are at the end of your investigation what is your answer to the question 'what was it like to live in the Roman Empire?'
2 What are the main differences between your first hypothesis and the one you have just described?
3 Why did you make, or not make, changes to your first hypothesis?
4 Do you think it is possible to make a simple statement, or put forward a simple hypothesis about what it was like to live in the Roman Empire? Explain your answer and provide examples to back-up the points you are making.
5 Is there a right answer to the question? Do you think that historians might disagree about the answer?

Oxford University Press,
Walton Street, Oxford OX2 6DP

*Oxford New York Toronto
Delhi Bombay Calcutta Madras
Karachi Petaling Jaya Singapore
Hong Kong Tokyo Nairobi
Dar es Salaam Cape Town
Melbourne Auckland*

and associated companies in
Berlin Ibadan

Typeset by MS Filmsetting
Limited, Frome, Somerset
Printed in Hong Kong.

INDEX

✤ Notes to teachers

Exercises offering opportunities for developing
pupils' understanding of the concepts and skills
required in the Attainment Targets, are
labelled as follows. Most of the questions are
linked firstly to the key concepts enshrined in
the Attainment Targets and most, but not all, of
the questions in the exercises are linked to
Statements of Attainment.

AT1a	Changes	15 43
AT1b	Causes and Consequences	46
AT1c	People in the Past	31 33
AT2	Different Views	37 42
AT3	Evidence	3 13 19 29 35 41

The accompanying Resource Pack includes
extension work, marking schemes and some
homework sheets.